ROOT OF SUFFERING

YOGI'S GUIDE TO OVERCOME SUFFERINGS

BRAHMAJNANI

गुरुर्ब्रह्मा गुरुर्विष्णुः गुरुर्देवो महेश्वरः ।

गुरुः साक्षात् परब्रह्म तस्मै श्री गुरवे नमः ॥

gururbrahmā gururviṣṇuḥ gururdevo maheśvaraḥ .

guruḥ sākṣāt parabrahma tasmai śrī gurave namaḥ ..

The guru is Brahmā, the guru is Viṣṇu, the guru is Maheśvara (Śiva),

the guru is the self-revealing limitless Brahman.

Salutations to that revered guru.

GURUVE SARANAM

Contents

Acknowledgements

Dedicating this Book to all my Masters (GURU's) who is guiding me each and every moment.

its my first Dream Book coming true , this book would not be possible without Ms.Rejina Shanthi mam (Counselling psychologist & clinical hypnotherapist) inspiration and Zubin sir's Genioustrainers - training . Thank you for your love and support .

Preface

GURUVE SARANAM

Welcome you all with love and blessings .

Before enter into the chapters , just wanted you to know , some of the basic truths to gain more from this book. you may know or may not know the information or concepts which is shared in this book . Generally , mind always function to acquire something new , it needs something new which is not heard of , which is not seen before , it needs something interesting to move further . early days in villages , rumours will spread more than forest fire , In modern days all social media's is the alternative for spreading rumours , That's why entertainment channels , videos , prank shows , TV serials are all going viral and trending . Even though everyone knows it's no use for our day to day functions ,even then mind needs some kind of entertainment,to pass the time .When compared to other entertainment activities like watching serials, watching movies playing games , watching some tele shows , Netflix , listening some music , habit of reading books is absolutely amazing , no doubt about it . But that doesn't serve the purpose completely .having information without working on it , is like having food without digesting it .Sometimes it may become danger for the health . What will happen , if food goes into our system and not digested ? its danger is it .

In Vedanta, there is the 3-fold process ,which leads one to complete Awakening and Realization. They are Shravana, Manana, and Nididyasana.

" **Shravana** " - means hearing , Hearing the Truth!

" **Manana** " - means contemplating the Truth

" **Nididhyasana** " - means living and breathing the Truth

So my humble request is to read , contemplate and apply it in your life . That will be the fruit of this Book . If , any ONE person applying it in life and get benefited out of this Book , it served my mission.

A small story: A learned scholar went to meet a Zen master . The scholar had done a lot of research in many areas of study. He went to meet the master to get some spiritual knowledge, to understand spirituality in a better fashion. He arrived at the master's place and found the master brewing tea. The master saw him and gestured to sit, and continued to brew tea. The scholar sat down and after a while, started talking of his background, of all his studies, his discoveries, his travels around the world, his experiences with different people, his conclusions on various subjects and what not. The master finished brewing the tea and placed two cups between them. He began pouring tea into the scholar's cup. He poured and poured and slowly the cup started overflowing. The tea spilt over the saucer and flowed onto the table. The scholar was watching what was happening. He could not contain himself any more. He screamed out, 'Master, what are you doing? Stop pouring! The cup is overflowing!' The master stopped and calmly said, 'So are you.' The scholar was shocked but understood what the master was trying to tell him. The scholar was so full like the tea cup! Anything that the master might tell him would only overflow outside, not into him. The scholar understood from that one word of the master, what he meant, what he was trying to tell him.

So understand: if you really want to gain something, just be like an empty cup here. Be totally open and receptive . that is enough. Tips to have more benefit out of this Book. Read , when you are free-mind or make your mid free to read . Read , as if you are reading first time , even if you would have heard these information earlier. If any techniques given try to implement it , in your life Read again and again , to make the information into knowledge and to experience . If you simply read once it will become information , when you read and contemplate on the truths it becomes knowledge , when you read , contemplate and implementing the truths , it becomes experience .

Author not claiming that , all information and ideas are entirely new and different , But it's all written after attain wisdom and spiritual experience in the field of body , mind , soul. It's not just information , it's an experience .

This book contains knowledge , truths and experiences extracted from various external world scientists (doctors, physiatrists, mentors, coaches) and inner world scientists (rishis , sages, enlightened beings and guru Parampara - guru-disciple lineage) .Hence its combination of truths from modern science and Traditional inner science (Hindu sanathana dharma) .

CHAPTER ONE

TO WHOM IS THIS BOOK FOR ?

This Book Is For You ... Yes, YOU!!!
It is the purpose of this book to tell YOU how to get rid of all sufferings in your life . Let's get it clear:
When this book says: "You", it means YOU (yes, YOU!!!)
This book is a complete PROVEN SCEINCE specifically for YOU—to enable YOU to get rid of root of sufferings .
This book is based on a great, old proverb: "The tide lifts ALL the boats." The tide does not lift only some boats or only special boats-it lifts ALL the boats.
This book is written for YOU . . . whoever YOU are wherever YOU are whatever. YOUR age whatever YOUR skin colour . . . whatever YOUR present education (or lack of education). whatever YOUR present situation (whether YOU are employed or unemployed) whether YOU are rich or only in the middle income bracket or poor .. whether YOU live in.

THIS BOOK IS FOR YOU (yes, YOU!!!) . . . .

My prayers and blessings to lift all the sufferings of ALL its readers. Let us understand some of very basic meaning for suffering , emotions, feelings before even going to the truths .

CHAPTER TWO

WHAT IS SUFFERING

Suffering, or pain in a broad sense, may be an experience of unpleasantness and aversion associated with the perception of harm or threat of harm in an individual. Suffering is the basic element that makes up the negative valence of affective phenomena. The opposite of suffering is pleasure or happiness.

PAIN is Positive existence in nature , but SUFFERING is Negative existence like shadow.

CHAPTER THREE

WHAT IS EMOTION AND FEELINGS

While emotions and feelings are quite different, we all use the words interchangeably to more or less explain the same thing – how something or someone makes us feel.

However, it's better to think of emotions and feelings as closely related, but distinct instances – basically, they're two sides of the same coin.

CHAPTER FOUR

WHAT ARE THE EMOTIONS

Imagine this:

You are going to the airport, on the run to catch your flight. While you try to make your way through the crowd of people waiting in line at the security check, you see an old friend you haven't seen many years .

Before you can say anything, you tear up overwhelmed with excitement (and forget about the rush) while you give your friend a firm hug.

Emotions are lower level responses occurring in the subcortical regions of the brain (for example, the amygdala, which is part of the limbic system) and the neocortex (ventromedial prefrontal cortices, which deal with conscious thoughts, reasoning, and decision making)

CHAPTER FIVE

WHAT ARE FEELINGS

While emotions are associated with bodily reactions that are activated through neurotransmitters and hormones released by the brain, feelings are the conscious experience of emotional reactions.

Originating in the neocortical regions of the brain, feelings are sparked by emotions and shaped by personal experiences, beliefs, memories, and thoughts linked to that particular emotion. Strictly speaking, a feeling is the side product of your brain perceiving an emotion and assigning a certain meaning to it .

Emotional stimuli are usually classified by considering two main dimensions: Valence, which describes the attractiveness (positive valence) or aversiveness (negative valence) of stimuli along a continuum (negative – neutral – positive), and arousal, which refers to the perceived intensity of an event from very calming to highly exciting or agitating .

CHAPTER SIX

HOW MANY EMOTIONS DO WE HAVE

Modern day Scientists experimented elaborate study on human feelings, emotions to find out how many are there, The patterns of emotion that they found corresponded to 25 different categories of emotion . which are : admiration, adoration, appreciation of beauty, amusement, anger, anxiety, awe, awkwardness, boredom, calmness, confusion, craving, disgust, empathic pain, entrancement , excitement, fear, horror, interest, joy, nostalgia, relief, sadness, satisfaction, and surprise.

Admiration - usually enthusiastic appreciation and often deep affection.

Adoration - deep love and respect

Appreciation - understanding and enjoyment of the value of something

Amusement - state of experiencing humorous and entertaining events or situations , and It is an emotion with positive valence and high physiological arousal

Anger - an emotion characterized by antagonism toward someone or something you feel has deliberately done you wrong.

Anxiety - a feeling of fear, dread, and uneasiness. It can be a normal reaction to stress.

Awe - feelings of respect and either fear or admiration.

Awkwardness-mean not marked by ease, and may suggest unhandiness, inconvenience, lack of muscular control, embarrassment, or lack of tact.

Boredom - state of feeling disinterested in one's surroundings, having nothing to do or feeling that life is dull.

Calmness - mental state of peace of mind being free from agitation, excitement, or disturbance. being in a state of serenity, tranquillity, or peace.

confusion - Inability to think or reason in a focused , clear manner

craving - a strong desire for something.

disgust - a strong feeling of not liking or approving of something/somebody that you feel is unacceptable, unpleasant.or something/ somebody that looks, smells, etc.

empathic - showing an ability to understand and share the feelings of another.

entrancement- a feeling of delight at being filled with wonder and enchantment. A feeling of extreme pleasure or satisfaction.

excitement - the state of being excited, especially because something interesting is happening or will happen

fear - an intensely unpleasant emotion in response to perceiving or recognizing a danger or threat.

horror - painful and intense fear, dread

Interest - feeling of a person whose attention, concern, or curiosity is particularly engaged by something

joy - a feeling of great happiness

nostalgia - a wistful or excessively sentimental yearning for

return to or of some past period or irrecoverable condition
relief -feeling that you have when something unpleasant stops or becomes less strong , the removal or reduction of pain, worry, etc
sadness - Feeling down or unhappy in response to grief, discouragement or disappointment
satisfaction - the feeling of pleasure that you have when you have done, got or achieved what you wanted; something that gives you this feeling.
surprise - the feeling that you have when something happens that you do not expect it can be neutral/moderate, pleasant, unpleasant, positive, or negative.

Understand , emotions are more like colours. Just as there are many different colours in between red and green—like yellow, orange, brown, laser lemon, electric lime, and so on—there seem to be many different emotions in between fear and disgust, Greed .

the researchers came with below conclusion that ,

Emotion: Scientists do not always agree on what makes up an "emotion," but they usually agree that it is more than just a feeling. Emotions can also involve bodily reactions, like when your heart races because you feel excited, and expressive movements, including facial expressions and sounds—for example, when you say "woah" because you are fascinated by something. And emotions can involve behaviours, like yelling at someone when you are angry. These bodily reactions, expressive movements, and behaviours are often included in scientists' definitions of "emotion."

Feeling: The way that someone experiences an emotion. A feeling is something that you experience internally, in your own mind, and that other people can understand based on your behaviour. You can help other people understand how you feel using emotion terms, like "anger" or "sadness"—the subject of this study—or by using analogies, like "I feel the way a kid would feel if her dad took away her Halloween candy."

Correlation: A measurement of the degree to which two things tend to rise and fall together. For instance, height is correlated with weight, because taller people are usually heavier.

CHAPTER SEVEN

WHAT SCRIPTURE'S SAYS SUFFERING

In Hindu theology, Arishadvarga are the six passions of mind or desire

kama — lust

krodha — anger

lobh — greed

moha — delusory emotional attachment or temptation

mada or ahankara — pride, hubris

matsarya — envy, jealousy

the negative characteristics of which prevent man from attaining moksha or salvation. Kama and krodha or lust and anger are responsible for all kinds of difficult, suffering experiences which we have in our lives. With mada or ahankar, the false ego up and active, all our acting in the world becomes selfish. Hence there is no other factor causing the illusory duality of differentiating between 'us' and 'them' and the repeated pain and delusion it entails than the psychological ego-sense. When the materially identified ego has sided with the materialistic forces of creation (Maya), it is said to have the following faults: kama, krodha, lobha, moha, mada and matsarya. Also called evil passions, man's Spiritual heritage constantly gets looted by these internal thieves (and their numerous variations), causing him to lose knowledge of his True Being.

If a person is virtually a prisoner of arishadvargas (the six internal enemies of kama, krodha, lobha, moha, mada and matsarya), then his life is totally governed by the destiny. As a person moves ahead on the path of Self-Realization, the grip of the destiny over him loosens and he gets more and more leverage to change his destiny. When a person identifies himself with the Self, then, he becomes part of the destiny power. His power of mere sankalpa is good enough to materialize and change any situation either for good or bad according to his sankalpa.

Karmic forces flourish when the individual is self centered. The thoughts of "I" and "Mine", one's indulges in Kama, Krodha, Lobha, Moha, Madha and Matsarya are tools of Karma to perpetuate worldly desires and objectives. Quietening the mind and turning contemplation towards Easwara are the two requirements to mitigate Karma.

Awareness of the self is what existence is all about. But the SELF is comprised of multiple components. The major components of the self are the Body, Mind, and consciousness. Mind and Consciousness, the chief components of perception and awareness and intelligence together are known as MANAS.

Like the ten heads of Ravanna, the mind is composed of many different parts, each of which wants the prime attention of one's consciousness.

The different parts of the mind could be physical and could be attributes.

Karmic forces flourish when the individual is self centered. The thoughts of "I" and "Mine", one's indulges in Kama, Krodha, Lobha, Moha, Madha and Matsarya are tools of Karma to perpetuate worldly desires and objectives. Quietening the mind and turning contemplation towards Easwara are the two requirements to mitigate Karma.

Awareness of the self is what existence is all about. But the SELF is comprised of multiple components. The major components of the self are the Body, Mind, and consciousness. Mind and Consciousness, the chief components of perception and awareness and intelligence together are known as MANAS.

Like the ten heads of Ravanna, the mind is composed of many different parts, each of which wants the prime attention of one's consciousness.

The different parts of the mind could be physical and could be attributes.

The physical aspects are directly the needs of the body and the organs in the body. So food, shelter, clothing, disease, sickness, coping with disabilities, reproductive needs, are all the needs of the body and consumes a lot of the attention of our conscious waking time, The mind's primary job appears to be to provide for the bodily needs by enacting its Karma in the physical world. This effort to preserve the physical does result in evolution since it involves development of skills to interact with people and objects.

This aspect is the outward turn of the mind. It has to deal with the physical aspects by acquiring knowledge of the physical world.

The other aspect of the mind are the attributes. The major attributes are Kammam, Krodham, Moham, Lobham, Madham, Matsaryam.

The above attributes are the ones that drive physical action to preserve the self. So essentially these inner aspects of the mind are a direct result of the interaction of the mind with the external world. Without these inner attributes the external world will have no impact and will not be able to influence the inner self.

There are a few other major attributes that are not entirely the result of the physical world.

These are very strange attributes that seem to completely control the mind and its boss - our consciousness

1. Ahankara or Ego This is aspect of the mind that is the separator of the self from all other observed phenomena in the world. So it is the official name for the "I" within the mind.

2. Chitta - Will power. This is an ability that has both physical and mental impact. It is the "ability" that enables us to move our limbs according to the dictates and requirements of the mind. This is also the power to keep the mind from wandering away and being subject to the pull of Kammam, Krodham etc. A very powerful attribute that needs to be consciously cultivated.

3. Buddhi - Intellect. This is the ability to relate our experiences to the primary cause. For example - the understanding that if we commit a crime, we have to face the consequences, or that if there is smoke, there is a fire somewhere. It is not just a matter of relating the physical events and occurrences to the causes. It can be very effective in understanding and controlling the working of the mind itself.

The aggregate of all the above individual heads is the MANAS and constitutes the centrepiece of Ravanna's 10 heads. The MANAS, being pulled in different directions by the different aspects of itself, becomes the Control Canter and tries to keep the reins on uncontrolled horses pulling in different directions and tries to steer the chariot in the correct direction.

So we are seekers of complete liberation from bondage. We are forced to seek liberation from the cycle of births and deaths and seek peace and tranquillity . The "I" represents the focus of these desires.

CHAPTER EIGHT

WHY DO WE SUFFER

A small story:

A man was known to have a very weak heart. His family was always careful in telling him any drastic news. One day, they came to know that his wealthy uncle had died leaving one million dollars to him. They were very excited and at the same time did not know how to break this news to him. They were afraid that he might collapse hearing it. One of them suggested, 'I think we'd better call the family doctor and tell him to handle this.' They all agreed. They called up the family doctor and told him the matter. The doctor said, 'Don't worry, I will handle it. It is not so hard as you think.' He soon arrived at their house and went into the room and started talking to the man. He casually asked him, 'If you were suddenly told that you were given one million dollars in cash, what would you do?' The man replied, 'I would give half of it to you, doctor.' The doctor collapsed and died.

Is suffering is your choice or your status mind

Most often even don't know suffering is a choice not a state of mind

so we suffer because we don't know how to handle this situation, how to handle the person, how to handle the incident ,

You should understand that suffering is state of mind, not state of life.

It's not real, it's happening because we choose to suffer, if we know the knowledge of living without suffering, then will chose that first.

Unfortunately we have been thinking that suffering is happens naturally in a given situation .but the reality is it's our choice to suffer. We can choose to suffer or choose not to suffer .

Now look at the question consciously

why do you have suffering,

When you fall sick ?

When your neighbour buy a car?

When your loved one fall in love someone else?

Most of our sufferings will fall in these categories only I.e. ....physical, psychological, emotional levels.

Now , if you decided to accept the reality as it's,

Without getting anger or vengeance.

not to get anger on your loved one ,

not to get jealousy on your neighbour,

Will you reduce the suffering or not?

Are your suffering will be in the same level?

Understand ,

suffering will come when you resist the reality.

How much ever you resist that much you suffer.

When you bringdown the resistance your suffering level will come down.

" Suffering is resistance to the present moment "

CHAPTER NINE

REASONS FOR SUFFERING

ROOT PATTERN IS THE MAIN REASON FOR ALL OUR SUFFERING

What is Root pattern :

The first strong cognition you receive in your life, which influences you to continue to function based on the same cognition, is a root thought pattern!

It is the pattern you develop when powerlessness takes you over for the first time in your life. Your pure cognition is imbalanced and your mind is born!

The way you behave, feel and respond, all come from this root thought pattern. It is the limiting cognition that happens in you and fills you at a very young age, overpowering you.

Sometimes it is fear, sometimes it is greed, sometimes it is jealousy and sometimes it is the decision to prove yourself. Sometimes, it is just plain confusion and worry!

A Small Story :

There are four young boys standing on the street ,suddenly a big cobra coming towards them , the first one got scared and ran away from that place , second one got scared instead ran away, looking some sticks here and there to beat and kill the snake, third one though he has some fear of snakes he don't want to kill the snake , he asking his friend to chase it aside , the fourth one standing coolly nearby the snake and clicking selfie with snake to post it on the social media .

What we need to understand from this story , the situation , the place , the snake , the people are all same but when you notice they are reactions on the situation is entirely differs from each other is it ?

Why is that because of ROOT PATTERN which is developed in their childhood .

CHAPTER TEN

YOU ARE RESPONSIBLE FOR YOUR SUFFERING

you are 100% responsible

Suffering happens when you invest too much emotionally, in other people or in external events.

After all, how much control do you have over them? Be your own source of inspiration. Don't mortgage your happiness to someone else!

Remember, you are 100% responsible for your own suffering and your own happiness. It is the hard truth!

A small story:

A disciple kept asking the master, 'Master, where is paradise?'

Finally one day, the master asked him, 'Do you really want to know?'

The disciple sat up and said, 'Yes!'

The master said, "Alright, my first disciple is in paradise. After saying these words the master closed his eyes and went into meditation.

The disciple knew it would be a long time before the master opened his eyes. So, he went and asked some of the disciples if they knew where this disciple lived. No one seemed to know. Finally one disciple said, 'I know how to guide you there, but I have never been there myself. It is in a deep valley beyond a range of ice covered mountains.'

The disciple wrote down the directions carefully and went back to the master. He told him, 'Master, I wish to pay a visit to your first disciple!'

The master was absorbed deeply in some work Without even looking up he said " Go ahead "

The disciple wrote down the directions carefully and went back to the master. He told him, Master, I wish to pay a visit to your first disciple!'

The disciple started on his journey. He walked for many days, passing through sun, rain, snow, and what not. He became exhausted, on the verge of death. It took him one hundred days to reach the valley. When he finally reached it he looked at the valley and thought, 'This valley doesn't look all that great. I have seen many more beautiful valleys. Why did the master call this paradise?

He looked around and walked further and finally found the first disciple's hut. The first disciple was very pleased to see him. He served him food and asked how the master and other disciples were doing.

All along, the disciple was thinking to himself, Master called this place paradise? / can't believe it.'

After a week-long stay he left and returned to his master. It took him another one hundred

The master said, 'Oh god! At the time of your enquiry, had you been more explicit about your intention, I would have told you the truth.'

The disciple asked, 'What is the truth?'

The master replied, 'He is not in paradise. Paradise is in him!'

When you see what is as it is, you are in heaven. When you want to see what you want to see, you are in hell. If you understand that everything is auspiciousness, you will drop expectation and see things as they are, because everything is auspiciousness.

CHAPTER ELEVEN

ATTACHEMENT BRING SUFFERING

Most of our suffering due to attached with something, attached with some person, attached with some place.
For example , there is a bird in your house and you are upbringing by feeding , taking care of it. and , in one day it dies because of Some climate situation or some accident .now you have a feeling of guilty that you didn't maintained it properly, having a suffering that, I killed that bird , I may get sin of killing that bird .
Now you suffering Not because of the bird died , actually you are suffering because of your attachment with the bird . If you are a person having suffering because of loss of any life ,
every day we are getting news that so many lives are killed , so many are dead in accident , in murder , why its not affecting you ? It's not because , it's happening somewhere else , it's because you are not attached with it.

Same way If someone dies in our family or close friend , we will have suffering So we are not bothering about the loss of life , we only suffering due to our attachment with people .
you thinking that I have the sympathy of loss of life, that is

why I am suffering is a myth.

You know every day so many lives or getting killed , so many are committing suicide

So many are getting Murdered but that doesn't shake you because you are not attached with them .

you are not suffering because you are not attached with them . if you are a person who is so loving, caring towards pet and animals, you can't eat the dead fish or mutton or anything which is lying in your plate.

But when bird dead, you are suffering it doesn't mean you are bothered about life , you are bothering because of attachment with the bird not out of care towards life.

you be very clear whether it is a person , whether it is a situation , whether it is a place

if something removed from you , you are suffering not because of the people are the life or the place ,you are suffering because of your attached with it.

Be very clear , you only care about your body, not about other beings.

You only care about your attachment not about the lives.

It's your attachment makes you suffer, not you care for other lives.

CHAPTER TWELVE

SUFFERING IS THE ROOT OF EGO

When you live close to Existence, without any expectation, seeing what is as it is and finding the blessings in it, you will carry heaven in you! Heaven is not geographical, it is psychological. It is not physical, it is mental. If you decide, you can be in heaven right now. Then the whole work becomes too difficult. It is like trying to work Your ego cannot exist without your suffering. Suffering is the root of your ego. This is an important thing you need to understand.

We always think that the ego is disturbed by suffering. No! Ego is enriched by suffering.

If your suffering is less, your ego feels it is too small! You feel you are too small, so you increase your suffering so that you can feel you are somebody. Many times you may have seen,

whenever someone says something to you the first reaction inside you is a certain resistance , a “No”. Usually , when you see something , you either try to identify it , or we try to condemn it. when you experience what you call as suffering , you either accept it or you try not to suffer! You never understand or go beyond suffering.

You can only understand only within your frame of reference , what you are familiar with . because of this , you are caught in a limited view of possibilities .to really understand you need to go beyond this limited point of view .to do that you have to stop naming it suffering, that's all!. There will no more suffering. Only by naming it, you start the conflict. That is how you see what IS – by not naming it.

A small story:

A man got onto a bus and sat down next to a young man. He could see that the man was a hippie. He was wearing only one shoe.

He asked him, 'You have lost one shoe?'

The young man

replied, 'No, I have found one shoe.'

Stop naming any situation, person, or thing! Just see, that's all. Don't give room for condemning or accepting thoughts. Initially there's a compulsion to pass judgment on anything that you see because that is your habit. But when you experience the great energy released in you by seeing what IS, you want to remain that way – free from thoughts, worry, and suffering.

CHAPTER THIRTEEN

SUFFERING CAN BECOME AN ADDICTION

Almost all the miseries you face in your life are knowingly or unknowingly created by you, to fulfil your vested interests. One of the most deeply hidden reasons for suffering is that you are enjoying it.

For example, falling ill can become a source of pleasure if it gets you the attention and care you have been craving. Some people love suffering so much that it becomes second nature to them. It is almost like a comfortable feeling.

You see, you sit in certain postures because it makes you feel very comfortable; that familiar cozy feeling. Same way, depression also gives you this kind of psychological cozy feeling, and without that you feel you are some way stiff or missing something.

That is how depression gets rooted in your system. Suffering becomes almost like an addiction. People are very happy with it. Without that they feel something is missing See, when your physical body is mature, it goes on giving birth to more and more bodies just like itself. Same way, if the pain body gets mature beyond a certain level, it goes on expanding, giving birth to itself. More and more and more pain bodies are created. When the pain body gets mature, it just goes on reproducing more and more pain bodies just like itself.

Catching the pain body, taking care that it does not become more and more mature, that it does not become like an addiction, is a very important thing.

CHAPTER FOURTEEN

TYPES OF SUFFERING

- Necessary Suffering

- Unnecessary suffering

A small story:

A husband and wife were celebrating their fifty years of marriage. The wife presented the husband with two shirts. He was very touched and declared that they would go out for dinner instead of cooking at home. It was a very tender moment for them. He freshened up and to make his wife happy, wore one of the gift shirts and appeared from his room. As he came down, she looked up and smiled, but soon her expression changed and she asked, 'So the other shirt is no good?'

In Mahabharata, there is beautiful quote by Kunti, the mother of the Pandavas. She prays to Krishna, 'O Krishna! Let pain and suffering come from all sides in my life. They will constantly remind me about you, my Lord.

Krishna, I want sufferings. I want pain. I want more sufferings and pain!

Why did Kunti ask for sorrow for her whole life as her wish to Lord Krishna in Mahabharata?"

See if we do not have any problems in life we will forget the lord , So if we have problems we will definitely preach/ seek god .That's why Kunti asked for sorrows so that she will not forget the god and she will be preaching him. She was a devotee of Lord Krishna and knew that he was the God himself in human form. That's why when Lord Krishna asked her to ask something from him, Kunti asked for sorrow all his life. Her logic was that human beings remember God the most when they are in trouble or sorrow and forget God when they are happy and comfortable. That's why she asked Lord Krishna for sorrow for her whole life so that she remembers God all through her life.

Understand :

Kunti did not ASK FOR SORROWS. (She asked for Necessary suffering)

The verse (Bhagavata Purana 1.8.25) reads:

vipadaḥ santu tāḥ śaśvat tatra tatra jagad-guro
bhavato darśanaṁ yat syād apunar bhava-darśanam

The translation is:

"Let there be difficulties again and again, o Guru of the universe. Because (in difficulties) we may have the opportunity to see you, and this means we will not have to take birth ever again." Difficulties are not sorrows.

Vipadah means "bad situation".

And saying "let there be" does not mean asking for something.

It means, "it's ok if they come".

We need to understand both necessary suffering and unnecessary suffering ,

Necessary suffering will leads you to transformation , unnecessary sufferings will leads you to lower level .

Start to witness your experiences without judgment. See with clarity where you are suffering at the gross and subtle levels. If you are just aware, the suffering itself can open your eyes to the unreality of suffering. It can teach unnecessary it is to suffer at all.

This is what call 'necessary suffering'! Once you learn your lesson through necessary suffering, you will handle suffering in mature and beautiful way.

Never curse the pain or the person inflicting the pain on you.

Instead, take the opportunity to use it as a blessing, watch objectively, and cut the root of the pain. Pain can be a great teacher if you allow it to be. If you properly research the cause and effect of pain within you, it can turn out to be the biggest turning point in you.

When you identify the necessary suffering and approach with right mindset, your life will be transformed like seed becoming plant , like caterpillar becoming butterfly.

catterpiller with butterfly

CHAPTER FIFTEEN

SUFFERING/WORRY DIFFERS EVERY PERSON

A small story:

A man walked into a bar looking worried and upset. The bartender asked him, What's the matter? You look very worried about something.'

The man said, 'My wife and I had a fight and she told me that she wouldn't talk to me for a month.'

The bartender consoled him, 'It's okay. One month isn't that long.'

The man said, 'I know. The month is up today!'

Everyone has his or her own set of worries! If I ask you what you worry about, you will tell me, 'I don't have a job, that's my worry. 'Your neighbour will say, 'My job is my main worry!' Someone else will say, 'My children are my worry.' Another person will say, 'I don't have children, that's my worry!' One person's dream is another person's worry! You will not find any logic in it at all.

What is meant by 'worry'? Worry arises whenever things are not happening as you want them to happen. It is the discrepancy between your expectations and reality. For example, you feel your son should stay at home with you, whereas he feels he should be by himself - away from you. You want to finish your project by a certain time. But things are happening too slowly and it seems an impossible task. These are all causes for worry. What you want and expect does not match what others want and expect

Small Story

A man and his friend were having a cup of tea together one evening. The man told his friend, 'I am planning to divorce my wife. She has not spoken one word to me in the past 6 months.' The friend said, 'Think carefully before making any such decision. You won't get another wife like that.'

CHAPTER SIXTEEN

HOW ROOT PATTERN DEVELOPS

WHY / HOW ROOT PATTERN (programming) DEVELOPS ?

Material nature consists of three modes or attributes: goodness(satva) , passion(rajas) and ignorance (tamas) . These are called Guṇas in Saṃskṛit.

Kṛiṣṇa explains in bhagavad gita , how we operate through three different types of root thought patterns.

One is SATYA, the other is RAJAS and the third is TAMAS.

These are translated as goodness, passion and ignorance; however, these are not exact translations.

Let us understand these concepts:

Satva - refers to the root patterns that lead us to bliss, the space of completion.

These root patterns lead us to joy and ecstasy.

Rajas - refers to the root patterns that lead us to restlessness, excitement and to work intensely. They make us active and materially productive.

The third attribute,

Tamas - refers to the root patterns that lead us to depression, laziness and to dullness.

Root patterns that lead to ecstasy and bliss form satva.
Root patterns that lead to restlessness, anger and emotional imbalance form rajas.
Root thought patterns that automatically arise and imbalance our cognition, and lead to depression, dullness, and low moods are called tamas.
Rajas and tamas are the reasons for us to go through all the sufferings (powerlessness)
Powerlessness developed from

Kama — lust ,
krodha — anger,
Lobh — greed,
moha — delusory emotional attachment or temptation,
mada or ahankara — pride, hubris,
matsarya — envy, jealousy.

When we entertain and associate ourselves with powerlessness, it is so powerful that it can destroy us. It's worse than alcohol and poison. Poison destroys our physiology.
Alcohol destroys our psychology. Powerlessness destroys both our physiology and psychology.

CHAPTER SEVENTEEN

HOW TO HANDLE OUR EMOTIONS

Recognise your strongest emotions Which emotions control your actions? Does your life revolve around hostility, aggression, and anger? Are you frequently depressed for no reason? Is it more important for you to love, or fight? Be honest with yourself!

You must first acknowledge your emotions – otherwise how are you going to transform them?

Even depression is nothing but anger turned upon oneself.

When you express the emotion, it is anger.

When you repress it, it becomes depression.

But both are the same negative energy.

When we focus on our negative emotions, when we nurture our sense of separateness,

when we create an experience of 'me versus them', the ego feels very powerful.

That's why many of us enjoy

situations where we can be in a fighting position.

The positive, softer emotions always make us vulnerable.

Love, joy, compassion – these are very fragile states of mind.

When we experience these emotions, the boundary between ourselves and the
world becomes weaker. The ego feels less powerful.
That's why we all are afraid of these emotions. In a deeply unconscious way, we are
afraid of love – because in love we have to surrender the ego.
But spirituality is nothing but the process of losing one's ego.
There is a small story about Buddha and his disciples:

One day Buddha arrived for his usual morning discourse with his disciples. He had a knotted handkerchief in his hand. He showed the handkerchief to the disciples and asked if any of them could come up and untie the knot.

One disciple went up and tried to untie it. He pulled and pulled and the knot tightened. Another disciple went up, he looked at the knot %r a few seconds and easily untied it.

All he did was look at the knot and immediately he knew how the knot was made in the first place. So, he just reversed the whole thing and untied it! The knot itself taught him how to untie it.

In life worries are the knots in the handkerchief. If we look at them with awareness, we will know how to dissolve them. We will see exactly how the worry was created and then know how to 'untie' it. The worry itself will teach us how to release it.

A small story:

One man prayed to god, "Oh lord, please have mercy on me. I work so hard while my wife stays at home. She enjoys staying at home while I slog the whole day. Please grant me a boon whereby I become my wife and she becomes me. I want to teach her a lesson on how tough a man's life is.

God granted his wish.

The next morning, the man who was now the woman, woke up early in the morning, packed lunch for the children, made breakfast, got the children ready and drove them to school. She then came back and put the clothes in the washing machine, went to the bank and cashed the checks, paid the electricity and phone bills. Next she went to the market and bought some groceries, put the clothes out to dry, picked up the children from school, sorted out all their problems, helped them with their homework, watched television and ironed clothes at the same time. Then she prepared dinner, fed the children, put them to sleep, had dinner and went to bed.

The next morning the man prayed to god again, "Oh lord, I don't think I can handle this tomorrow. I beg you to please switch me back to a man.

God replied, "Of course I will switch you back to yourself but you will have to wait nine months because you are now carrying a child!"

Each individual plays an equal part in life. No one should be taken for granted. There has to be some gratitude for every person on planet earth. I always tell people that even if things don't work out between you and your wife and you have to part, part with gratitude.

The problem is that somewhere we feel people are waiting to hurt us. It is not so. It is only our own insecurity which we project on others.

CHAPTER EIGHTEEN

HOW TO COMPLETE

How to do Completion process (erase/reprogramme)

Step one : BY REALIZING ABOVE TRUTHS :

A small story:

Three fisherwomen went to sell fish one day and it became late that night when they were returning home. They decided to spend the night in some house on the way. They entered the house of a lady who sold jasmine flowers for a livelihood and they requested to spend the night there. The lady agreed and they went to sleep in the room given to them. The house was filled with the fragrance of the jasmine flowers. But however hard they tried, the fisherwomen could not sleep. They were tossing and turning, and they did not know what to do. Then suddenly, one of them got up, brought in the empty fish basket and kept it by their heads. They went to sleep in no time

realize that each of our thoughts, words, and activities arises from one of the three root patterns, guṇas—satva, rajas and tamas.

Step Two : By understand and Regagnise :

understanding about which guṇa, root pattern it is and exactly what that guṇa is doing to us; what disempowering cognition that guṇa is building about our inner image (mamakāra), our outer-image (ahaṁkāra), others' image (anyakāra), others' expectation about us, and life's image (svānyakāra).

A small story:

A man goes to a psychiatric doctor and says, 'Doctor my life is full of problems'. The doctor says, 'Everybody's life is a problem. Don't worry. Every week we will have three sessions and you will be charged hundred dollars.' The man says, 'Doctor three sessions per week each at hundred dollars will solve your problem. What about my problem!' Understand, the moment we start believing that the mind is only a machine, we become helpless. No psychiatrist can help. No psychoanalyst can help. No other method can help, because the basic belief is wrong. The moment we bring a wrong belief, whatever is built on that has to go wrong. It cannot be the truth. We need to understand the basic truth that the mind is a process; we are not in tension but we are tension.

Step 3 : By Completion Process :

Do the completion and the creation process; do completion with that guṇa or root pattern and do creation of the satva guṇa, the right inner space to create the reality that we want.

Finally we transcend satva guṇa and enter into nirguṇa or 'no guṇa state'.

Every one of you has a fantasy deep down about you becoming all-powerful, all-knowing,

living as per the expectations of you, behaving as you expected about you, is the greatest joy

you can experience in life. Completion does that to you!

nothing else can do that to you.

One's IDENTITY is the collection of one's root patterns, saṁskāras, past bio-memories and incomplete desires that are stored in the unconscious mind. This is in the causal layer of our energy.

Through deep and focused meditation, and completion process we can access this unconscious causal layer and dissolve the saṁskāras stored here. Once done, we no longer return as the same person. We are free of saṁskāras and liberated.

CHAPTER NINETEEN

TECHNIQUE TO REMOVE ROUTE PATTERNS

A small story:

Two friends went to a cinema theatre to watch a newly released film. One of them noticed that the other was frequently looking at his watch. Finally he whispered to him, 'Are you not enjoying the film?' The friend replied, 'I am. I am just wondering how much more time is left to enjoy.' Most of us are like this! We are so tuned to worrying, that even if there is nothing to worry about, we worry about how long this state of no-worry is going to last!

Your problems are like a Grass called NUTSEDGE , Deep routed.

How much ever a former works on weeding those grass called nutsedge, by cutting it on the surface or through fertilizer will not possible to get out from the nutsedge , and it will ruin all properties of the soil and stop harvesting.

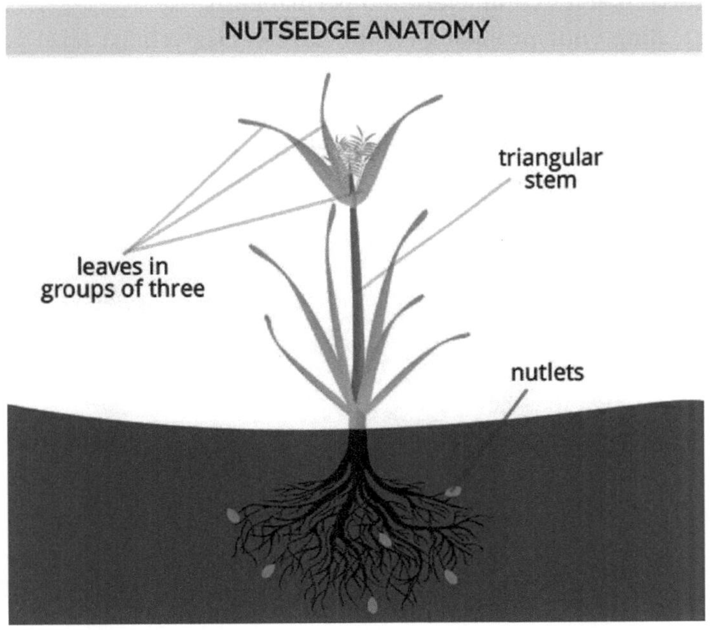

Nutsedge with Nutlets

He knows that there is deep routed NUTLETS at end of the root of nutsedge, until unless it's taken away from the agriculture land, it will grow again and again and again....
So the only solution is taking out those nutsedge along with nutlets.
Yes, of course it needs lot of time and energy with the patience to do it.
Your sufferings also has to be dealt with the same way, by understanding all your problems are deep rooted called root patterns. Until unless we able to identify

those root patterns you will not able to come out from the problems completely and permanently.
Dealing your problems on the surface, superficial level is like watching motivational videos, reading related to body and mind, going for a retreat program , attending and practicing some mind coach techniques , understanding about neuro linguistic etc., ...

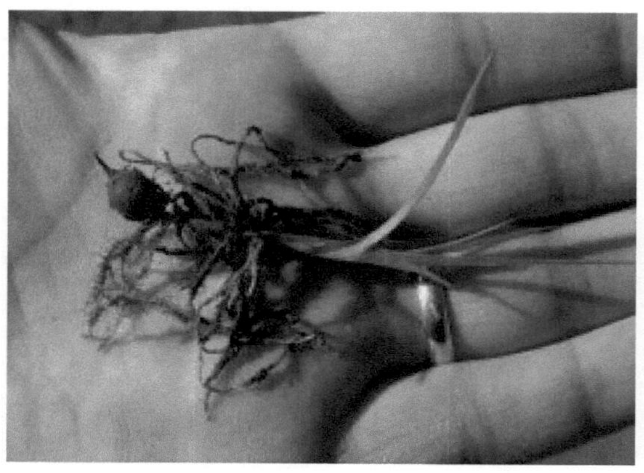

Nutsedge with Nutlet

It may give some solution immediately but it will not long lasting permanently. It's only a temporary solution.
You need to work on your deep routed root patterns which is accumulated in our body and mind over the period of time from the childhood.
All you need
TIME ,
ENERGY,
PATIENCE,
COMMITMENT,
WILL PERSISTENCE.

AND most importantly a person who knows about root patterns and ability to remove it
is called MENTOR/GURU/MASTER . HOW TO DO COMPLETION: (it needs someone's guidance in the beginning)
Just for twenty-one days, every night before sleeping do self-completion with all your incompletions for at least forty-two minutes; reliving and relieving your past sufferings and root patterns. This completion process will directly work on your causal layer.
just by completing with your past lifestyle, you can get out of all your sufferings of the past.
Just by declaring completion with all the past mental setup, you can get out of all the side effects, after-effects, and impact of the past over you. So, completion forms the basic truth, the basic principle. The whole energy field supports you to fulfil your life as you want.

Say NO to suffering

Below is a simple but powerful meditation to experience the space of non-suffering:

INSTRUCTIONS

Sit for a few minutes with this one truth: 'I will not suffer.'

Decide consciously, 'I will not allow my husband / wife / anybody else to torture me and give me suffering. I will not allow anything to give suffering to me. Non-suffering is my birth right .'

Take this as a religious decision.

DO THIS FOR ATLEAST 12 DAYS , YOU WILL SEE THE MIRACLES IN YOUR LIFE I WILL PRAY FOR YOU ALL TO ALMIGHTY TO REMOVE ALL YOUR SUFFERING AND ACHIEVE THE PURPOSE OF THE LIFE WHICH IS EXPERIENCE SUPER CONSCIOUS

BREAKTHROUGH .

LOVE & BLESSINGS

About The Author

BRAHMAJNANI

Level 1 : THE WORLD AROUND ME (Living in the culturescape)

I was born and brought up in a very small village in Tamil Nādu south part of India , lived cozy comfort life based on the parental conditions and societal conditions. without knowing anything about self, life, world ....

Graduated in Bachelors of business administration (BBA) at the age of 21, Masters in Business Administration (MBA) at the age of 23 and Semi-qualified chartered accountant at the age of 25 .few years worked as an accountant in Chennai .

Level 2 : THE WORLD I CHOOSE

During my teenage , I had lost my father, i realised that this is not the life as I want, it's not my choice, started contemplating myself, reading books of enlightened masters like Osho, G. Krishnamurthy, Paramahamsa Yogananda, Ramakrishna Paramahamsa, Swami Vivekananda ,Swami Nithyananda , Vedathiri Maharishi and many others.,

from then my life had lot of ups and downs

Started my spiritual journey (inner journey) to explore myself, to understand the purpose of life, to experience the ultimate consciousness .

I understood my life should not be an ordinary human life , I decided to choose the life as I want to live without conflict in and around me .

Level 3 : THE WORLD INSIDE YOU (Recoding yourself)

Fortunately , Gifted to take birth in south INDIA, Tamil Nadu .
being born in a place where thousands of enlightened masters, siddha's, incarnations, rishis (INNERWORLD SCIENTISTS) happening time and then to transfer the knowledge to achieve each and every BEING , which is ONLY the purpose of life (not only human being) knowingly ENLIGHTENMENT / SUPER CONSCIOUS BREAK THROUGH / GOING BEYOND MIND / ETC.,
met various enlightened masters, attended spiritual programs , visited various pilgrims with the seeking to achieve enlightenment.

Pending the reality

- World will say renunciation is running away from the responsibility

experienced renunciation is not the outfit of the society, it's overfit from the society.

- World will say life is only about Take birth ,educate , acquire wealth, build relationship (marriage...?!) ,have children's, die at the end.

renounced family, friendship, relatives, qualifications, societal conditions at the outer world and recode myself from the lust, anger, depression, anxiety, mood swings and all other incompletions.
Took sanyas (monk) under a living master served around him for the past fifteen years.

Level 4 : THE WORLD I CAN CHANGE (Becoming extraordinary)
Realised and experienced myself that every human being has enormous energy within us that's inner potency to handle ourselves and others. And spread the possibility, positivity to the world .

Now I am in the mission of reaching out the soulmates to spread the happiness, Heal the body mind and consciousness, inside and outside around the Globe .

Understand if you are reading this Book , there is a reason .

it will be revealed at the right time .
your birth has some reason , you will achieve soon.

Love and Blessings
BRAHMAJNANI .

BRAHMAJNANI SRI NATESHANANDA

9 798886 295504

Printed by Libri Plureos GmbH in Hamburg,
Germany